Just the Facts

Cocaine

Sean Connolly

Heinemann Library
Chicago, Illinois

Designed by M2 Graphic Design
Printed in Hong Kong / China
Originated by Ambassador Litho Ltd.

05 04 03 02 01
10 9 8 7 6 5 4 3 2

Library of Congress Cataloging-in-Publication Data
Connolly, Sean, 1956-
      Cocaine / Sean Connolly.
        p. cm. – (Just the facts)
      Includes bibliographical references and index.
      ISBN 1-57572-255-0 (library)
      1. Cocaine habit—Prevention—Juvenile literature. 2. Cocaine habit—United States—prevention—Juvenile
literature. 3. Cocaine—Juvenile literature. [1. Cocaine 2. Drug abuse.] I. Title. II. Series.

HV5810 .C7 2000
362.29'8—dc21
                                                            00-026790

Acknowledgments
The Publishers would like to thank the following for permission to reproduce photographs:
Camera Press: pg.12, pg.13, pg.18, pg.41, Julian Hawkins pg.14; Corbis: pg.25; David Hoffman: pg.33, pg.43; Frank
Spooner: pg.38; Gareth Boden: pg.50; Images Picture Library: pg.10; Impact: Keith Bernstein pg.19; Magnum Photos:
pg.11, Abbas pg.6, Susan Meiselas pg.26, pg.34, Fred Mayer pg.46; Mary Evans Picture Library: pg.21, pg.23, The
Coupland Collection pg.30; Meg Sullivan: pg.48; Peter Misrlow: pg.40; Rex Features: pg.5, pg.7, pg.8, pg.28, pg.29,
pg.31, pg.44, pg.45, pg.49; Science Photo Library: pg.17; Stuart Franklin: pg.20, pg.22; The Stock Market: pg.37.

Cover photograph reproduced with permission of Tony Stone.

Every effort has been made to contact copyright holders of any material reproduced in this book.
Any omissions will be rectified in subsequent printings if notice is given to the publisher.

Our special thanks to Pamela G. Richards, M.Ed., for her help in the preparation of the book.

Some words are shown in bold, **like this.** You can find out what they mean by looking in the
glossary.

Contents

Introduction

Cocaine is a drug that has always had a great deal of publicity. Much of its reputation rests on the fact that it is expensive and that it is a popular drug with the rich and famous. It is often associated with fast-moving people. This reputation is a major reason that many people are tempted to take cocaine; they hope that they, too, will share in this experience.

Mystery and misunderstanding

Like many abusive drugs, the reputation of cocaine has changed with the times. Along the way, the form of the drug itself has changed as well. From its humble roots as a mild **stimulant** found in the the coca leaf, cocaine was developed as a cure-all medicine. When its medical usefulness fell out of favor, it was widely recognized as a health menace. That view was largely abandoned during the 1960s, when cocaine was naively viewed as a relatively harmless alternative to other, harder drugs, such as heroin. Finally, during the 1980s, a more potent variety of cocaine was developed. Known as crack, this drug soon became widely recognized as the most dangerous drug available.

This book sets out to put cocaine in its proper historical and medical perspective. Powdered cocaine, for example, is not a harmless drug, a view held by many users during the 1980s. And while crack does not necessarily turn first-time users into instant **addicts,** as many people believe, it does have the power to destroy lives very quickly. Like any abusive drug, the high that cocaine provides comes at a heavy price. It is important to realize that the price is not only calculated in terms of money, but also in lives ruined and even lost.

A user prepares several lines of powdered cocaine. He will use the rolled up bill to **snort** the cocaine into his nostrils.

What Is Cocaine?

Cocaine is a white, crystal-like substance that usually appears in powder form. Its chemical name is *cocaine hydrochloride,* and its street names are *coke, Charlie,* and *snow.* Most street cocaine contains only 45 to 50 percent of the drug. The rest usually consists of a filler substance, such as sugar. The highly **concentrated** crack cocaine, which is also known as *stone, rock, base,* or *freebase,* consists of 85 to 95 percent pure cocaine crystals. Both cocaine powder and crack are illegal drugs, and people caught possessing or selling them can face severe penalties. In schools with **zero tolerance policies,** students found possessing illegal drugs, such as cocaine, are immediately expelled.

South American roots

Cocaine is taken from the coca plant, which has two distinct species. *Erythroxylum coca* grows in the tropical forests on the eastern slopes of the Andes Mountains in South America. The second species, *Erythroxylum novagranatense,* grows in the drier mountainous regions of Colombia, along the Caribbean coast, and in some dry parts of Peru.

It is still common to see coca leaves on sale in the village markets of the Andes in South America.

The effects

Cocaine powder is a **stimulant.** Stimulant drugs seem to provide extra energy and confidence to those who take it. The effects are more intense than those of similar drugs called amphetamines, but they do not last as long. When taking cocaine, a user feels **euphoric,** confident, and serene. In addition, the user experiences a heightened sense of alertness and a decreased sense of pain.

A number of dangerous physical effects accompany the cocaine high. These include raised blood pressure, heartbeat, and body temperature, as well as a decreased need for food and sleep.

Cocaine users feel these effects soon after the drug is taken, the first feeling is usually a sense of exhilaration or excitement. The effect soon levels off, and most of the common effects, such as increased confidence and alertness, take hold. The cocaine high lasts about 40 minutes. When it wears off, the user often feels agitated, depressed, tired, and **paranoid.**

How people take cocaine

The many South Americans who use the coca leaf do not use it to achieve the effects normally associated with cocaine. Rather, they have used it for thousands of years to alleviate the difficult conditions associated with living at a high **altitude.**

The cocaine sold illegally on the streets, which comes as an odorless powder, is usually inhaled through the nose, or **snorted.** The cocaine user inhales the drug quickly through a tube. This process can be quite painful, and many people feel an intense irritation in their nasal passages.

When users snort cocaine, the drug enters their bloodstream through the soft tissue of the nostrils. It takes a little while for the cocaine to dissolve and seep into the blood stream. Aside from the dangerous effects of the drug, continued cocaine snorting can cause serious health problems. For example, the soft tissue of the inner and upper nostrils can decay, damaging the tiny blood vessels that lie just below the surface. Heavy cocaine users often have frequent and serious nosebleeds as a result. Despite such side effects, most cocaine users prefer to snort cocaine rather than to **inject** it, a practice that carries the risk of contracting **hepatitis** or the **HIV** virus.

The cocaine habit is expensive because it encourages the user to take more of the drug to maintain or prolong the high sensation. It creates in the user a compulsion, or intense desire, to take more of the drug, which adds to the already high cost of obtaining a single dose.

Prevalence

Cocaine has always been an expensive drug, and this fact contributes to its attraction. Many modern users misguidedly view cocaine as a status symbol, an activity that demonstrates wealth.

The present pattern of cocaine use began during the late 1960s, when pop stars began to take the drug. Earlier in the same decade, the most popular **stimulants** were amphetamines. However, word soon got out that cocaine provided a smoother high. Cocaine use peaked during the mid-1980s, when 10.4 million Americans reportedly used cocaine. In contrast, by 1998, an estimated 3.8 million Americans used cocaine at least once per month.

Because of its perceived status, cocaine is used by a relatively small portion of young people. However, cocaine use by young people has increased during the past 10 years. According to the U.S. Department of Justice, in 1991, 2.3 percent of eighth-graders said they tried cocaine. By 1999, that figure had risen to 4.7 percent. In 1991, 2 percent of students in grades eight through twelve had tried crack. By 1999, 3.9 percent of students in that age group had tried the drug.

Dance culture

Although cocaine use among young people is small compared with some other drugs, anti-drug professionals worry that it will increase further. Since the early 1980s, drug-taking has been a major part of the youth dance club scene. Unfortunately, like dance steps, certain drugs come in and out of favor with the crowds.

Since about the mid-1980s, Ecstasy had been the most popular dance drug; however, during the mid-1990s, users became concerned about the purity of the drug being sold on the street. Drug users feared that they were buying a more dangerous drug. Amphetamines, illegal drugs that provide an energy boost similar to that of Ecstasy, are gaining favor on the club scene, with cocaine following behind. Because cocaine is more expensive than other drugs, some young people are dangerously mixing it with less expensive drugs, such as cannabis and hashish.

Crack Cocaine

Crack cocaine is a **derivative** of cocaine powder that produces an exaggerated version of the normal cocaine high. In fact, crack is like a more intense version of cocaine in every sense—the high, the sense of **dependence** it produces, and the psychological side effects.

Intense sensation

Crack is often called *freebase* because the drug's potent base, or active ingredient, has been extracted from the salts and other chemicals of cocaine powder. The result is far more powerful than cocaine powder. However, without salt, crack does not dissolve in water or become absorbed in the body the way that cocaine powder is. That means that crack cannot be **snorted** or **injected** effectively, so people smoke it instead. People often smoke crack in pipes made from soft-drink cans. The name *crack* comes from the crackling sound the crystals make when they are heated and burned inside the pipe.

Everything about crack happens fast. The rush starts immediately, begins to wear off in just a few minutes, and ends after about twelve minutes. As with cocaine powder, in order to get high again, the user needs to take another dose of the drug.

Cause for alarm

Crack became well known during the early to mid-1980s, when stories of its use began to spread. One of the most dangerous aspects of the drug was its ability to create **dependence** in the user after only a few *hits,* or uses. Exaggerated news stories described how people became crazed **addicts** after taking the drug just once. From its beginning, use of crack was concentrated in inner-city neighborhoods with high unemployment and few opportunities for recreation. The blast of confidence offered by crack was a short-term escape from the problems of life in a tough neighborhood. Unlike cocaine powder, crack seemed to be especially popular with young people.

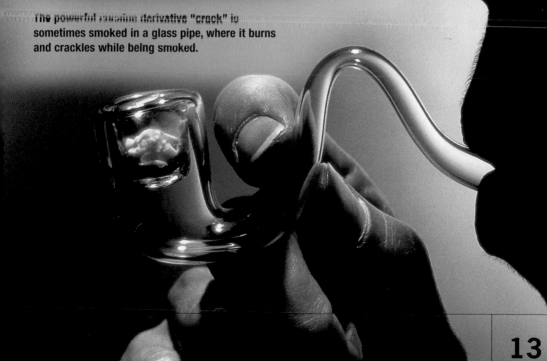

The powerful cocaine derivative "crack" is sometimes smoked in a glass pipe, where it burns and crackles while being smoked.

Links to crime

The original claims about crack that "one hit and you're hooked" are exaggerations, but there is no denying that crack takes hold of people in a way that powder cocaine does not. The problem of **dependence**—the urgent need to get frequent supplies of crack even when there is no money to pay for it—creates the problem of crime.

Many crack users turned to robbery to get money for more of the drug. Young people used abandoned houses or apartments as a base, or crack house, and went out in search of money and more supplies. Then they returned to take the drug. During the 1980s, U.S. newspapers were full of stories about the crack **epidemic,** and fear spread about a new generation of **addicts** unleashing a fearsome crime wave.

Crack remains a serious problem, both in terms of drug dependence and of crime. However, there has been a move away from the use of crack, especially among the young, inner-city people who previously had been the most frequent users. People in many inner-city neighborhoods have made it clear that they do not approve of the way in which crack has threatened their young people. For many crack addicts, this local pressure to stop taking the drug is more powerful than the criminal **prosecution** they face for selling the drug.

❝It got to the stage where I wanted crack so badly that I would crawl on the floor for crumbs (of the drug), it made me feel so alert, like I was the best person in the world and the world is a good place—for three minutes—and then you have to have more. I'd come down crying and feeling terribly lonely.❞

(Sam, former crack user, quoted in *Drugs Wise* by Melanie McFadyean)

Cocaine and Addiction

Although the terms **addictive** and **addict** are often used in relation to drugs, most medical professionals prefer the terms *dependent* and *dependent user.* Part of the reason for this slight change of terms has to do with social perceptions: the word *addictive* carries a sense of being uncontrollable and even unforgivable. *Dependent,* on the other hand, suggests a way of behaving that can be overcome. Professionals also find it useful to talk of someone being either physically dependent or psychologically dependent on a drug.

A drug causes physical **dependence** if the user continually needs to increase the dose to maintain the effects—a pattern called **tolerance**—and then suffers **withdrawal** symptoms when it is stopped. Alcohol and heroin are good examples of drugs that cause physical dependence. Cocaine, with the possible exception of crack, is unlike these drugs because it does not promote physical dependence.

Cocaine craving

For many years, drugs workers focused their efforts mainly on drugs that caused physical dependence. Therefore, many people wrongly considered cocaine relatively harmless. However, the medical community has known for many decades that cocaine can lead to a profound psychological dependence, in which the mind craves the good feelings that come with the drug. Furthermore, the fatigue and depression that many users feel after stopping the drug—although not textbook withdrawal symptoms— encourage further use.

Cocaine users often begin craving the drug, or yearning for the pleasant effects of the cocaine high. Over time, these cravings intensify, leaving the user unable to deal with daily routines without cocaine. Some users are unaware of these changes, although many users recognize how the drug has come to dominate their lives. The increasing cost of the habit is one obvious signal. However, cocaine users also notice they are giving up or reducing their social or family activities because of the drug.

A regular cocaine user will often snort many lines of the drug in a single session in order to recreate that first rush of being high.

Cocaine tests

Scientists have carried out tests on animals to measure a user's intense need to have cocaine. If rats or monkeys are trained to press a lever to deliver an **intravenous** dose of cocaine at will, they will keep on pressing for up to three hundred times for a single dose. If they can reach a large supply of cocaine, they will continue taking it until they have **seizures**. In similar tests involving heroin or alcohol, the animals would not take enough to kill themselves; however, they would do so with cocaine if the scientists had not stopped them. Such experiments have been discontinued because of concern for animal welfare; however, they did shed light on the power of cocaine.

"If I had been in a room full of cocaine, I would have kept using it until it was all gone, and I still would have wanted more."

(Anonymous cocaine addict, quoted in *Buzzed* by Cynthia Kuhn)

Crack—a special case

Crack had been publicized during the 1980s as a drug that produced instant dependence after just one hit. Such stories have now been proven false. However, it would be dangerous to drop all concerns about this form of cocaine. Crack produces a high that is far more intense than that of cocaine powder, and the craving for a repeat experience is also stronger. Coupled with the fact that the effects of crack wear off after just fifteen minutes—after which many users want another hit—crack cocaine can easily foster a **binge** pattern of use. It is among the only drugs that can make a person spend $2,000 a week on supplies.

Cocaine and pregnancy make a dangerous mix. Regular cocaine users often give birth to premature babies.

Cocaine's History

Both cocaine and crack cocaine **derive** from the leaves of the coca plant, which grows at high **altitude** in the Andes of South America. It is believed that Native Americans in that region chewed coca leaves as early as 2500 B.C., although the first recorded use dates from around the sixth century A.D. Pictures of people chewing coca leaves are seen on pottery and other **archaeological** relics from that era. These early users had discovered that the chemicals in the coca leaves reduce fatigue and **suppress** hunger —important **assets** when living and traveling in the difficult high-**altitude** conditions of the Andes.

Spanish discovery

When Spanish soldiers conquered the Inca Empire of the Andes during the sixteenth century, they found that coca-leaf chewing was an important part of the society there. In addition to its energy-giving aspects, coca was a vital part of Inca religious ceremonies. The Spaniards viewed this as a **pagan** practice, totally at odds with their own Catholic religion. As a result, they tried to ban the use of coca-leaf chewing.

Native Americans in the Andes have chewed coca leaves for centuries to gain energy for coping with life at such high altitudes.

The Australian surgeon Karl Koller's use of cocaine as a painkiller helped to introduce the drug to the medical world.

The Spaniards, however, needed the labor supplied by the same local people, and they saw how chewing coca leaves enabled these people to continue working. This ability was particularly important in the vast gold and silver mines operated by the Spaniards, so they relaxed their hostility to coca use. Today, poor miners in Peru and Bolivia still use coca as a substitute for food to get them through the day.

European reaction

For the next two hundred years, travelers to South America returned to Europe with favorable reports about coca. Some even brought back **specimens** of the coca leaves to demonstrate how they worked. Two factors stood in the way of coca's acceptance in Europe. The first was pure manners: many Europeans did not approve of the chewing and spitting involved. More importantly, however, coca leaves simply did not travel well. Unlike coffee, for example, they were dry and useless after the long ocean voyage across the Atlantic.

The first cocaine

This changed during the mid-nineteenth century. In 1855, German chemist Friedrich Gaedcke isolated the active drug in the leaves; four years later, another German, Albert Niemann, improved the **process** of producing the drug.

Both of these chemists saw cocaine as a drug with medical value. However, it was only during the 1880s that medical scientists recognized the power of cocaine. In 1880, Russian doctor Vasili von Anrep noted that there was no pain from a pinprick when cocaine was **administered** under the skin. German and American scientists began to take an interest, and by the end of the decade, they had made many claims about the benefits of cocaine. In addition to cocaine's painkilling qualities, they cited the way the drug excited the body's nervous system. Ironically, some doctors even believed that cocaine could be useful in treating alcohol and morphine **dependence.**

Misguided medical claims

One of the most famous scientists to conduct research on cocaine was the Austrian Sigmund Freud, who later became known as the father of **psychoanalysis.** In 1884, Freud published the paper, *On Coca*, the first real study of cocaine. Freud argued that regular use of cocaine could cause weakness and moral decline, but that these factors were outweighed by its benefits to medicine.

Freud later withdrew many of his claims about cocaine, and the medical community also began to grow concerned about cocaine dependence and the risk of **overdose.** Despite this increasingly negative view by doctors themselves, many products containing cocaine reached the market and were sold as cure-alls without medical evidence.

❝All other observers affirm the view that the use of coca in moderation is more likely to promote health than to impair it.❞

(Sigmund Freud's early, misguided view of cocaine, from *On Coca*, 1884)

Sigmund Freud saw cocaine as a useful medical aid, although he also noted the drug's negative effects on the mind.

The Clampdown

Although there were many cocaine-based cures and soft drinks on the market, the public remained fascinated by the drug. By the end of the nineteenth century, however, stories had begun circulating about people suffering cocaine **overdoses** and becoming dependent on the drug.

Strong reaction

U.S. and European authorities decided to take action against cocaine at about the same time early in this century. In 1914, the United States introduced the Harrison **Narcotic** Act, which imposed restrictions on all products containing cocaine. Britain's Dangerous Drugs Act of 1920 had similar aims. The British law was also a reaction to stories that during **World War I**, Germany was trying to encourage cocaine use among British soldiers.

A second wave

During the 1920s, cocaine use became illegal in most countries. However, it remained popular among small groups of artists, musicians, and other creative people who felt isolated from society in general. Musicians in particular used it, and by the 1950s, cocaine use was common among many jazz musicians.

Cocaine was not one of the drugs most widely used during the famous drug years of the 1960s, but by the early 1970s, the youth climate had changed. Once more it was musicians—in this case, rock musicians—who led the wave of cocaine use. By the 1980s, cocaine was a popular drug. In 1985, there were an estimated 12 million cocaine users in the United States alone, many of them **ambitious,** young, urban professionals.

Cocaine's reputation took a dive after some highly publicized cocaine deaths and poisonings in the United States. However, as the overall use of cocaine powder declined, crack was becoming a problem in its own right. Law officials have been intent on preventing the widespread use of crack because of their concerns about **dependence**-related crime and the effects it has on urban communities.

Coca-Cola (right) originally contained cocaine and was sold as a way of gaining extra energy.

> **❝I was impressed to see a man put a bit of charlie (cocaine) in his spliff (marijuana cigarette). It said the man must be doing well.❞**
>
> (British drug researcher Janaka Perera, talking about London in the early 1970s)

The Cocaine Cartels

The illegal U.S. cocaine trade grew after **Prohibition** ended in 1933. Prohibition was a nationwide law that made it illegal to sell or buy alcoholic drinks. It was a hard law for U.S. officials to enforce, and a network of **organized crime** developed to distribute illegal supplies. When alcohol became legal again, many of these criminals simply switched the focus of their illegal activities from alcohol to other drugs, including cocaine. By the 1940s, it was illegal to possess cocaine in all but two states. The nationwide network for distributing cocaine was already in place when the drug had its revival during the late 1970s and early 1980s.

Cocaine sources

Many criminals became rich from the cocaine trade, and various law-enforcement agencies around the world still struggle to contain the traffic. It is easier to transport compact material than bulk goods, so much of the cocaine reaching the United States and Europe has already been **processed** in South America.

Since the 1980s cocaine boom, several South American countries have dramatically increased production of coca. Peru now leads the world in coca production, with crop yields jumping from 5,442 tons (4,937 tonnes) in 1980 to more than 250,000 tons (226,800 tonnes) in 1991. Bolivia (90,700 tons, or 82,300 tonnes) and Colombia (72,560 tons, or 65,800 tonnes) follow. It is in Colombia, however, that most of the coca is processed into cocaine, and therefore the most profitable part of the world trade is centered there.

Villagers take the coca leaves to a central point, where the first stage of processing cocaine begins. Sometimes the leaves are dumped into a large swimming pool, which is used as a giant **refining** tank. This stage produces a coca paste, which is used for cocaine production. When about 2,000 pounds (900 kilograms) of coca paste have been produced, it is taken by airplane to the final processing centers in Colombia.

During the 1980s, groups of powerful Colombian drug dealers controlled four-fifths of the world's cocaine trade. They used violence and bribery to maintain their vast fortunes. Together, these groups became known as the Colombian **cartels.** The most powerful drug baron, Pablo Escobar, was headquartered in the city of Medellin, and at one point had a fortune estimated at $2.6 billion. In 1993, Escobar was shot dead by Colombian drug enforcement officers who had stormed his secret hideaway. Other people, however, continue the drug trade.

Roundabout route

Cocaine **traffickers** use a complex route to get the cocaine from Colombia to markets around the world. Shipments have been seized in Argentina, Brazil, the West Indies, Florida, North Africa, and the Netherlands. Some cocaine, particularly supplies destined for crack production, is smuggled by air. Cocaine traffickers use women known as *mules* to take two- or four-pound packets of cocaine to Europe from the East Coast or the West Indies. Cocaine is **processed** into crack in secret laboratories in the destination country.

This is one attempt at smuggling that failed. The traffickers' aircraft ran out of fuel while being chased by government agents.

The U.S. Drug Enforcement Agency predicted that the U.S. market for cocaine would become **saturated** in the early 1980s, and that exports to Europe would increase. That prediction seems to have been accurate. Spain and Portugal have become the main entry points for the European cocaine trade. In 1987, for the first time, amounts of cocaine seized by British customs officials outweighed those of heroin. By 1991, twice the amount of heroin had been seized, and the pattern has continued.

Pablo Escobar (with mustache) was the most powerful international cocaine dealer of the 1980s. Like other South American dealers, he flew large quantities of cocaine to the United States in light airplanes.

Escobar's fortune

Pablo Escobar, leader of the Medellin cartel, had enormous power and wealth. It was said that his first criminal activity was stealing gravestones and then re-selling them with new inscriptions. He came to dominate the cocaine trade, and his **assets** eventually included a fleet of 250 aircraft, 200 apartments in Miami, hotels in Colombia and Venezuela, and a private zoo. He was arrested in 1991, but spent his time in a luxurious prison that he had designed himself. Known as *Hotel Escobar,* it featured two hot tubs, a sauna, an exercise machine, and the latest office equipment to let him keep in touch with his employees. Escobar escaped from this prison in 1993 and was eventually shot dead in a Medellin suburb.

Who Takes Cocaine?

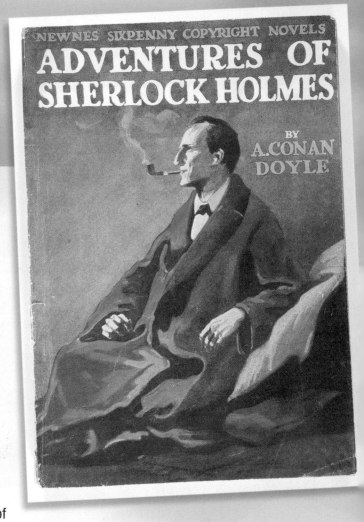

Cocaine is sometimes described as the rich person's **recreational** drug and the poor person's treat. This description ties in with its reputation as an expensive drug. It is also one of the drugs—like opium, alcohol and, to a certain extent, heroin—that have been given some glamour by appearing in famous books and songs. In Sir Arthur Conan Doyle's *Sherlock Holmes* stories of the late nineteenth century, the famous detective took cocaine in order to keep his mind sharp for solving cases.

The drug is also featured in songs, ranging from Cole Porter's *I get a kick out of you* (which begins, "I get no kick from cocaine") of the 1930s, to Eric Clapton's *Cocaine* of the 1970s.

> **❝I suppose its influence is physically a bad one. I find it, however, so transcendentally stimulating and clarifying to the mind that its secondary action is a matter of small moment.❞**
>
> (Sherlock Holmes, in *The Sign of Four*, 1888)

A wider market

Although such literary and musical references publicize use of cocaine generally, they also reinforce the drug's image as a luxury for the **elite.** The biggest change in attitude—and one that set the pattern for today's cocaine use—came during the 1980s. It was something of a **stereotype** to think that all cocaine users in that decade were high-flying professionals working on Wall Street or in other major cities. These young people seemed to live mainly for money. They believed that because they made so much money, they could afford expensive cocaine.

Moreover, the way in which these people viewed cocaine paved the way for a much wider use of the drug. In the past with cocaine, users either got high or went about their business. There was no way of combining the two aims. Young professionals and others during the 1980s believed that not only could they **snort** cocaine and then go back to work, but they felt that their work actually improved. But this behavior exacted a huge price.

Cocaine's allure

Some of the attitudes about the drug remain today. One of these is the sense that cocaine has an almost magical power to improve various aspects of life, ranging from creative work to romance. This view is based on hearsay and reputation, which for some people are more persuasive than the many reports that prove that performance in these areas actually suffers. Nevertheless, the image only reinforces the view that cocaine is an elite drug.

Another misconception is that cocaine is safe and not **addictive.** Compared with the worst aspects of alcohol or heroin abuse, cocaine may seem harmless. In truth, however, cocaine can lead to serious problems of **dependence** as well as a string of medical and psychological side effects.

Using cocaine

No two cocaine users follow the same pattern of behavior, and the fact that many people are able to build use of cocaine into patterns of work or study makes it even harder to come up with an image of a typical cocaine user. Crack, on the other hand, is much more immediately addictive. A typical day for a crack user would include a cycle of getting high, desperately seeking more of the drug, and getting high again—often linked with crime to fund supplies.

The behavior of a user of cocaine powder is linked to how heavy their use is. For a more habitual user, however, cocaine becomes a necessary part of the day. Such a person relies on cocaine to face up to the most routine challenges, such as getting through a day at the office.

Availability of Cocaine

The cost of cocaine—which is more than six times higher than amphetamines—makes it too expensive for drug users who have little spare cash. However, drug users with the cash and the determination to buy it usually succeed. Unlike heavily dependent heroin users, whose poor physical condition makes them easy targets for **unscrupulous** dealers, cocaine users remain attentive. Drug networks usually lead occasional users to dealers.

Purity

Cocaine is expensive for dealers themselves to buy, so they extend their profits by diluting, or mixing, cocaine with a number of other less expensive substances. This dilution process continues with each link in the chain of dealers before it reaches the streets. Some of these dilutive substances, such as amphetamines, might be **psychoactive,** which means they have an effect similar to pure cocaine. Other substances, such as novocaine, mirror the **anesthetic** qualities of cocaine. Still others—including cornstarch, talcum powder, and flour—might simply be the right color.

The end result, regardless of what has been added along the way, is that street cocaine is only about 40 to 60 percent pure. Crack, because of the further **refinement** that takes place to produce it, is anywhere from 80 to 100 percent pure.

Cocaine Consequences

Using cocaine regularly can have serious effects, not just on the individual user, but on the user's friends and family. Two aspects of cocaine that play a large part in the way it affects these relationships are its cost and the way it can lead to **dependence.** Very often these two elements are linked. Regular use of cocaine often takes a toll on household income. If the main money-earner is taking a lot of cocaine, other expenses tend to be ignored, and debts can mount. Furthermore, the need to finance a heavy cocaine habit can lead to a life of crime.

Deteriorating families

Regular use of cocaine brings with it a slew of other problems, which have even further effects within a family or friendship. Dependence on the drug often makes users behave in a way that hurts those around them. It dominates the users' way of thinking and seems to occupy their time, money, and attention.

This behavior leads to an atmosphere of distrust and suspicion. Friends and family members often feel hurt and abandoned when a loved one begins to spend so much time alone or with other drug users. This sense of abandonment can deteriorate a family. Even worse, the confidence-building nature of the cocaine high often prevents the user from recognizing that a problem exists.

Aggression, paranoia

The distortion of reality associated with cocaine use also triggers a number of other effects that harm relationships. Cocaine, like other **stimulants,** leads many people to become aggressive or **paranoid.** Cocaine users come to feel that the world is against them, and they react angrily to criticism or even simple requests. This, in turn, leads to a higher degree of physical violence on the part of cocaine users than is reported for non-drug users.

Whole families in Los Angeles have taken to the streets in protest against the use of cocaine and other drugs among young people.

Cracking up

The effects and consequences of crack cocaine are similar to those of cocaine powder, but are much more intense. A great deal has been written about the disastrous effects of crack on family life. The main problem associated with crack is the enormous cost required to finance a developed habit. Mounting debts, constant brushes with the law over thefts, and violence become realities for the crack user, and often shatter families.

Sometimes crack users band together to use drugs in places called crack houses. A crack house might be an apartment or abandoned building where people with very little in common meet. There is no real relationship among the people who go there, apart from smoking the drug, looking for more of it, and then suffering the after-effects together.

Calculating the cost

The street price of cocaine averages about $100 per gram in the United States. Each gram of cocaine contains enough of the drug for a user to sniff about ten *lines*. A light user of cocaine might get through about 0.25 gram in that period, although heavy users might consume 1 to 2 grams a day. So the heavy user could spend as much as $75,000 per year to feed the drug habit.

Legal Matters

In the United States, cocaine is controlled under the Comprehensive Drug Abuse Prevention and Control Act of 1970. It is illegal to possess or supply it to other people. It is also illegal to produce, import, or export cocaine, or to allow premises to be used for its production or supply. The U.S. Drug Enforcement Agency (DEA) lists cocaine among the most serious drugs of abuse in Schedule 1 of its drugs classification. Penalties for cocaine possession range from between 5 and 40 years in prison plus a fine for a first offense, to 10 years to life plus a fine for a second offense. In Britain, cocaine is controlled under the Misuse of Drug Acts of 1971. Federal laws in Australia also put cocaine in the most strictly controlled category of illegal drugs.

Heavier penalties

Anti-drug laws in most countries have more severe penalties for drug production and trafficking than for possession of drugs for personal use. In the United States, for

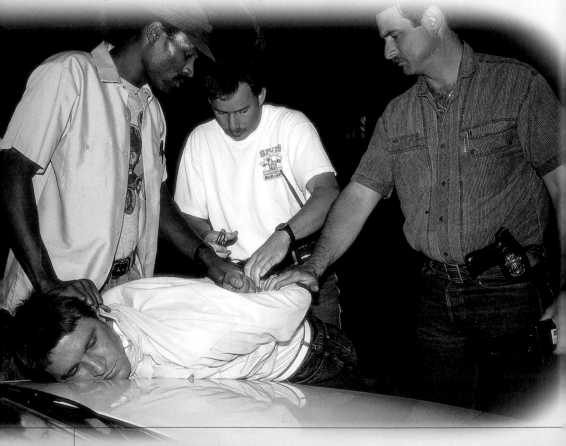

Special police dogs are trained to detect hidden supplies of cocaine, even when there are many competing smells.

Controlled Substance Act

The Controlled Substances Act (CSA), Title II of the Comprehensive Drug Abuse Prevention and Control Act of 1970, is the legal foundation of the United States government's fight against the abuse of drugs and other substances. This law is a consolidation of many laws regulating the manufacture and distribution of narcotics, stimulants, depressants, hallucinogens, steroids, and chemicals used in the unlawful production of controlled substances.

example, the maximum sentence for trafficking cocaine is five years' imprisonment for a first offense and ten years for a second offense, along with a fine. If trafficking results in a person's death or serious injury, it can lead to a sentence of life imprisonment as well as a fine. In the United States, penalties are more severe for the possession and trafficking of crack cocaine than they are for its powdered form.

School zero tolerance policies

Many schools throughout the United States have devised their own policies to control drug use on their premises. Under their so-called zero tolerance policies, any student caught possessing or selling any illegal drug can be immediately expelled from school. Such zero-tolerance policies exist in many U.S. workplaces and sports organizations as well.

Life with Cocaine

There is a substantial price to pay for the kick that cocaine provides. Some of the effects arise from just a single dose, while others develop over longer-term use of the drug. The most common physical effects are dry mouth, sweating, loss of appetite, and increased heart and pulse rate. Sometimes people who have sniffed cocaine feel a cold, numb, or burning sensation in the nose. This has to do with cocaine's properties as an **anesthetic.** Cocaine also causes the blood vessels in the nose to contract. As the effects of the drug wear off and the blood flow resumes, many users feel the symptoms of a bad cold—runny nose and general nasal irritation.

Deeper effects

More regular users report other physical effects. They often have a buzzing in the ears, diarrhea, tightness in the chest, insomnia, exhaustion, and an inability to relax. The increased heartbeat might become **chronic** or irregular. Crack smokers might suffer from constant coughing, wheezing, and even a partial loss of voice. Most cocaine users experience only a mild increase in blood pressure and slight heart pounding. If the drug has been used repeatedly over several hours or in one large dose, the blood pressure and heartbeat might shoot up, or the heart might start skipping beats. At this stage, the user faces a risk of **cardiac arrest** or **respiratory** collapse. Raised blood pressure leads to special problems for pregnant women. Taking cocaine during the later stages of pregnancy carries the risk of a possible heart attack to the mother. It might also lead to a small or underweight baby, who could have problems feeding or withstanding infections.

Cocaine is traded on the streets in a simple paper envelope called a wrap.

Injecting cocaine attracts the risks associated with injecting any type of drug, including **abscesses** and blood clots. Sharing needles increases the chance of contracting **hepatitis** or **HIV.** Many people who inject cocaine are also heroin users, and sometimes they inject a mixture of the drugs known as a speedball. This combination can be lethal. In fact, it accounts for the largest share of cocaine overdose deaths in the United States.

Cocaine-induced psychosis

Regular cocaine use can lead to a serious condition called cocaine **psychosis.** People suffering from this become **paranoid** and suffer delusions about what others are saying about them. Once the person has given up taking cocaine, and the drug is out of the system, the normal mental outlook returns. However, this recovery can take from several weeks to a few months.

Hollywood hazards

The fast-paced, high-earning lifestyle of Hollywood has often been linked with cocaine use. The early 1980s saw disaster hit two of its leading stars—both comedians—who were regular cocaine users. Each of them wanted a more powerful high, and each paid a disastrous price. In 1980, Richard Pryor was experimenting with a way of producing freebase cocaine, or crack, at home. The **process**, which involved heating up cocaine with an unstable solvent, went wrong and caused a huge explosion. Pryor was nearly blown apart and suffered extensive burns. He later said that he had been trying to commit suicide.

John Belushi had also been seeking an extra high. He injected a heroin and cocaine mixture known as a speedball. The effects are meant to be stronger than those of either drug on its own, but using speedballs masks the warning signs that precede an overdose. Belushi suffered this fate and died as a result.

❝I get a lot of cocaine through my boyfriend, who's in the music business. I feel suicidal quite a lot. I've tried to kill myself four or five times.❞

(Sarah, a 16-year-old regular user, quoted in *Drugs Wise*)

Richard Pryor (far left) and John Belushi (far right) are two well-known cocaine casualties in Hollywood. Belushi's experience proved to be fatal.

Treatment and Counseling

The best person to recognize cocaine **dependence** is the user. Although cocaine users often fail to realize that they are growing increasingly dependent on the drug, there are a number of warning signs. Drugs counselors and therapists often detect these warning signs by asking certain questions, some of which appear below:

- Do you ever use cocaine to help you function better?
- Do you ever feel guilty about your cocaine use?
- Have people ever confronted you about your cocaine use?
- Have you ever missed school or work because of cocaine use?
- Do you ever feel you'd do *anything* to get cocaine?

Other family members are often involved in a person's struggle to overcome cocaine dependence. They, too, are asked questions, including:

- Has the user's cocaine habit ever become a source of conflict?
- Is the user withdrawing from drug-free family and friends?
- Have money or expensive items ever disappeared from your house?
- Do you ever lie to others about the user's cocaine habit?

These are only some of the questions that should be considered by both users and family members, but it is worth noting that a *yes* to just *one* of these questions usually signals a problem.

Calling on others

Most major cities operate counseling services for drug dependence and provide referrals to other medical organizations. Cocaine's grip is almost exclusively psychological, so users need to have a clear idea about the sort of approach that suits their personalities. **Abstinence** is the stated goal and often the first step in most forms of therapy. After that, the drug user must decide whether to go for individual counseling or to join a group, such as **Narcotics** Anonymous.

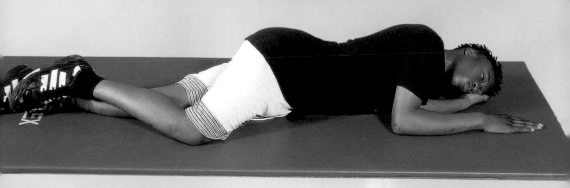

Overdose response

The most serious risk associated with cocaine use is **overdose.** The first signs of an overdose are a sudden rise in body temperature, a flushed face, hot but dry skin, cramps, and stiffness in the arms and legs. These symptoms occur when cocaine has increased the heart rate but closed down the blood vessels that allow heat to escape. If you witness such a situation, it is important not to panic and to call an ambulance immediately.

A drug user suffering an overdose should be cooled down by loosening the clothing and putting wet towels on the head and around the neck. The person should not be allowed to eat or drink anything except sips of cold water. If the person becomes unconscious, he or she should be turned on to one side on the floor (the Recovery Position), with nothing around to make him or her feel crowded. The overdosing person might start to convulse. In that case, it should be ensured that he or she does not hurt him or herself, but the person should not be touched until the convulsions are finished. Then, the person should be coaxed into the recovery position and watched until the ambulance arrives.

The Recovery Position, with a person lying freely to one side, is the safest way to look after someone who might be suffering from an overdose.

The Betty Ford Center (right) offers help for people with alcohol and other drug addictions. The Center was founded by Betty Ford, wife of the former President Gerald Ford. Ford herself was treated for alcoholism.

Open-air therapy

The Alliance Cocaine Treatment (ACT) Program, based in New Mexico, makes the best use of its dramatic mountain setting to deal with cocaine-dependent people. Like several other drug-treatment systems, the ACT approach is based on what is called the Therapeutic Community approach. In this technique, participants who had previously focused almost solely on themselves learn the benefits of working in a team.

In a series of such physical activities as rope climbing, white-water rafting, and mountain climbing, participants grow to appreciate the values of trust and communication. The goals set by participants of the program mirror the challenges they face in the outside world, the most important of which is living without cocaine. In the process, participants realize how much their actions affect other people

PROBST BLDG.
KIEWIT BLDG.
OUTPATIENT SERVICES
WRIGHT BLDG.
ANNENBERG CENTER
BETTY FORD CENTER

People to Talk To

While the negative effects of cocaine might not receive the frequent, dramatic headline reserved for heroin or ecstasy overdoses, they are profound. Because the effects of cocaine—the **paranoia,** the risk of overdose, the **psychosis,** and **dependence** on the drug—are less widely publicized, some people are misled into thinking that the drug is safe. As a result of this and of pervasive pressure from drug-using friends, many young people might be tempted to try cocaine.

Find a voice of reason

There are people to talk to who can put things in a different perspective, either by giving first-hand accounts of their own drug experiences or by outlining the clear dangers of cocaine abuse. It is best to turn to parents and older family members first. Unfortunately, many young people feel that they have little in common with their parents. Even sympathetic teachers and other local authorities, such as clergy or law enforcement officials, might seem too close to home.

In the United States, young people can call a wide range of telephone numbers to find out more about cocaine. Many of the numbers are toll-free, and most are anonymous. Whether you approach one of these organizations, a family member, a youth leader, or a teacher, the important thing is to be able to talk—and listen—openly about your drug concerns. Sharing a problem or worry is the first step toward solving it.

Information and Advice

The United States is well served by organizations providing advice, counseling, and other information relating to drug use. The contacts listed on these pages are helpful springboards for obtaining such advice or for providing confidential information over the telephone, on line, or by mail.

Child Welfare League of America
440 First Street NW
Washington, DC 20001
(202) 638–2952
The Child Welfare League of America, based in Washington, provides useful contacts across the country in most areas relating to young people's problems, many of them related to drug involvement.

Cocaine Anonymous World Service
P.O. Box 2000
Los Angeles, CA 90049
(310) 559-5833

DARE America
P.O. Box 775
Dumfries, VA 22026
(703) 860–3273
Drug Abuse Resistance and Education (DARE) America is a national organization that links law-enforcement and educational resources to provide up-to-date and comprehensive information about all aspects of drug use.

Youth Power
300 Lakeside Drive
Oakland, CA 94612
(510) 451–6666, Ext. 24
Youth Power is a nationwide organization involved in widening awareness of drug-related problems. It sponsors clubs and local affiliates across the country in an effort to help young people make their own sensible choices about drugs and to work against the negative effects of peer pressure.

More Books to Read

Carroll, Marilyn. Cocaine and Crack. Berkeley Heights, N.J.: Enslow Publishers, Inc., 1994.

Jaffe, Steven L., ed. Introduction by Barry R. McCaffrey. How to Get Help. Broomall, Pa.: Chelsea House Publishers, 1999.

Mass, Wendy. Teen Drug Abuse. San Diego, Calif.: Lucent Books, 1997.

Peck, Rodney G. Crack. New York, N.Y.: The Rosen Publishing Group, Inc., 1994.

Salak, John. Drugs in Society: Are They Our Suicide Pill? Brookfield, Conn.: Twenty-First Century Books, Inc., 1995.

Taylor, Clark and Jan Thomson Dicks. The House that Crack Built. San Francisco, Calif.: Chronicle Books, 1992.

Turck, Mary C. Crack and Cocaine. Parsippany, N.J.: Silver Burdett Press, 1990.

Glossary

abscess collection of pus in or on the body

abstinence going without something, such as drugs

addict person who is dependent on a drug

addictive cause to become compulsively and physiologically dependent on a habit-forming substance

administer dispense, as in to give a dose of a drug

affirm declare positively or to add weight to an idea or opinion

altitude height of a place above sea level

ambitious eager to advance in a career and to earn more money

anesthetic causing loss of feeling without loss of consciousness

archaeological relating to the study of historical remnants from other cultures

assets valuable items or qualities

binge short period of excessive use of a drug or other substance

cardiac arrest stoppage of the heart

cartel combination of independent business organizations formed to regulate production, pricing, and marketing of goods by the members

chronic lasting for a long period of time or marked by frequent recurrence, as in certain diseases

clarifying make clear or easier to understand

concentrated reduced in bulk or volume by the removal of a liquid or agent of dilution

dependence physical or psychological craving for something, such as a drug

derivative compound or substance derived or obtained from another and containing essential elements of the parent substance

derive develop from something else

elite small percentage of a population who has special advantages, such as wealth or power

epidemic wide-scale outbreak of a disease or social problem

euphoric characterized by intense feelings of happiness or well being

federal relating to the U.S. government. A federal law is one that applies to the whole country and not just its individual units, such as states.

hepatitis serious inflammation of the liver caused by infectious or toxic agents

HIV retrovirus that causes AIDS (auto-immune deficiency disease)

impair cause to diminish strength, value, or quality

inject pump into the body, usually with a syringe

intravenous taken by a needle into a vein

narcotic addictive drug, such as opium, that reduces pain, alters mood and behavior, and usually induces sleep or stupor

organized crime large-scale criminal activities

overdose dose of a drug that is too much for the body to absorb

paranoid characterized by the extreme fear or distrust of other people

peer pressure pressure from friends of the same age to behave in a certain way

Prohibition period between 1920 and 1933 in the United States when alcoholic drinks were considered illegal

process prepare by going through a special procedure

prosecution act of bringing a criminal charge against a person in a court of law

psychoactive affecting the mind or mental process, usually used to describe a drug

psychoanalysis study of a person's mind by exploring the unconscious impulses, anxieties, and internal conflicts

psychosis severe mental disorder characterized by derangement of personality and loss of contact with reality

refinement change of something by refining it

refining chemically purifying a substance

respiratory related to the act of breathing

saturated overflowing, filled, or loaded to capacity

seizure sudden attack, spasm, or convulsion, as in epilepsy or another disorder

snort to take cocaine by inhaling it through the nose

specimen individual item that represents the whole, such as a species of animal or plant

stereotype description of a group of people that stresses what are often assumed to be (sometimes mistakenly) their shared characteristics

stigma mark of disgrace

stimulant drug that makes people more alert or energetic temporarily

suppress lessen, as in the desire for food

tolerance decrease in the response to a drug after prolonged use

trafficker drug dealer who takes drugs across international borders

transcendentally mystically or supernaturally

unscrupulous dishonest or untrustworthy

withdrawal negative physical effects of giving up a substance

World War I war that took place between 1914 and 1918 between Britain, France, and their allies, and Germany, Austria, and their allies

zero tolerance policies policies enacted in schools whereby students found with drugs are immediately expelled

Index